FLUTE ARTISTRY

By Dylan Cramer

Publisher: Dylan Cramer
Musical examples: Liz Kinnon
Cover design: Riley Cramer

PREFACE

The esteemed Italian conductor Carlo Maria Guilini, when asked to describe what made Jasca Heifetz stand out from all the other violinists of his time, said the following: "Quality of sound, virtuoso technique, interpretation; these three qualities one must possess in order to have the highest musical character." And so it is true for the flutist. The quality of sound must instantly grab the listener; the finger technique must be of the highest efficiency; and the interpretation must be flawless.

Unfortunately, the majority of flutists around the globe are unable to fulfill these three requirements for flute artistry. Their sound is unattractive and often shrill; their fingering is haphazard and undisciplined; and their interpretations leave the audience feeling cold and emotionless.

However, there is hope. Thanks to two brilliant men, Henry Lindeman and Phil Sobel, a method that addresses these issues has been created and refined over the last 100 years. While Lindeman began the genesis of this approach in New York in the 1920s, Sobel continued it in Los Angeles for decades until his passing in 2008. Fortunate to be one of Sobel's students myself, I have carried on the method through my teaching and am now honored to present it, for the first time, to the flute community.

It is my strongest belief that anyone who applies the ideas in this book will not only revolutionize their thinking about the flute and music in general, but will ensure that their flute playing is full of the kind of sound, technique, and interpretation that are essential to revealing the nature of this most beautiful instrument, the flute.

Dylan Cramer
January 2025

HOW I STUDIED THE FLUTE

A saxophone player since the young age of 13, I became a flute player four years later through necessity. Working in a big band at one of the premier nightclubs in the town where I lived, I had the opportunity to work with several international headliners who came to play at the club. One of those headliners was the singer Al Martino, who arrived for the gig armed only with his charts and his pianist/conductor, Alberto Oliveri.

Oliveri was a short little Italian with a fiery temper which matched Martino's (it appears that Martino was forever disgruntled about passing on the song "Strangers In The Night" and held a lifelong grudge against legendary singer Frank Sinatra when he took it on and made it a hit). Upon meeting both of them, I found them to be rude, condescending, and irascible. To make matters worse, after checking out the saxophone book, I discovered there were many flute parts in it, and, as I did not play flute, I became rather nervous. Reluctantly, I approached Oliveri and asked him what I should do about it. Oliveri's response was to stare me down, scowl and then yell, "Well, *LEARN IT!*" And so, after a quick crash course to survive the gig, I began a love affair with the flute, which, at the time of this writing, has been a 50-year courtship. *Long live the Italians!*

Three years later, at age 20, I started studying saxophone, flute and clarinet in Los Angeles with Phil Sobel. Sobel, an LA studio giant, played lead alto for the NBC Orchestra for 18 years. He worked with the best of the best, including Sinatra, Luciano Pavarotti, and Ray Charles. But more than that, Phil was a gifted teacher. When I started working with Phil he was in his early sixties, vibrant, passionate, and deeply committed to both performing and teaching.

I worked with this amazing teacher from 1978-1986. Although the alto saxophone was my main instrument, my lessons always included flute and clarinet, something Phil demanded all his students do, with the hope that at least some of them would follow in his footsteps as a studio musician.

Unfortunately, I didn't connect with the clarinet at all and the clarinet didn't connect with me either. However, I did enjoy the flute, and progressed steadily on it, thanks to Phil's genius as a teacher.

I remember my first lesson with Phil like it was yesterday. Despite the fact that I expected to study saxophone with him, the first time I walked into his studio I only had my flute with me. On the music stand was a single sheet of music. "Play," he ordered.

The opening of the piece was a simple two bar phrase of three quarter notes followed by a dotted-half. I played the phrase but then he stopped me. "Do it again," he commanded, "but this time, *pick your fingers up slower.*"

And so, I did. Suddenly, I felt a strange sensation in my fingers and my sound. Startled, I stopped playing.

"Tuesdays at 10," he barked, slamming the door behind him.

What followed was eight grueling, insightful years under Phil's masterful direction. Phil pushed me hard, harder than anyone ever had, demanding my best at all times. No lack of concentration or effort was allowed in Phil's presence – and no excuses. Initially, I was afraid of him, but after about six months I realized that Phil was totally dedicated to make me the best musician I could be, and that he *truly cared*. It was at that time that I really began to flourish under his tutelage.

Of course, there comes a time when the student must move on from the teacher and head out into the world on his own, in search of himself and his artistry. After eight years with Phil, that time presented itself to me, although leaving him was a gut-wrenching decision. To this day, some 39 years later, I still find myself wondering if I made the right choice in leaving, which is an indication of the immense power Phil had over me. He was a brilliant, once in a lifetime teacher, never to equaled, never to be replaced, never to be forgotten.

Upon my return home to Canada, I decided to focus all of my musical energy on the alto, and began my recording and teaching career. I quit playing clarinet almost immediately but continued to play the flute as a secondary instrument.

As the years passed, I started to become bored with helping my students study the same band books year after year after year, and so I decided to do two new things: I took up the piano so that I could provide accompaniment for them, and I started using my flute (instead of my saxophone) when playing along with my saxophone students.

The old saying "Necessity is the mother of invention" soon took shape. Because I was now playing the flute with Eb and Bb saxophone books, I was forced to learn how to transpose, which, while challenging at first, became easier and easier, mostly through endless repetition.

Shortly thereafter, I started playing along with symphonic recordings from the classical masters (Beethoven, Brahms, Mozart and Tchaikovsky my most preferred). I focused on the violin parts, but I also played any and all of the other instrumental parts, transposing as I did so (Tympani on the flute? Oh yes, indeed). Because of the natural, relaxed sound the flute offered, I found it easy to jump from one part to another, although my initial attraction to the violin parts never left me (as I found them to be the most interesting and challenging). Playing along with the orchestra was a tremendous learning experience for me and completely revolutionized my flute playing and understanding of music. I experienced stunning insights into the use of dynamics, nuance, phrasing, blending, and vibrato (or lack of it), while simultaneously absorbing the superlative genius of these incredible compositions the masters left behind. It was, in short, a musical epiphany for me and a real breakthrough in my development as an artist.

I also played many pop, rock and jazz songs on my flute. Playing other musical genres helped me break free from the confines that playing only classical music can bind one to, and it gave me a greater appreciation for the unlimited musical styles in which the flute can prosper.

Now, decades later, a typical practice session on flute will start with an intriguing exercise or two, followed by whatever symphonic piece calls to me that day.

Next up is a lovely walk around the neighborhood, where I delight in observing the many beautiful elements nature provides, combined with the happy sounds of children frolicking in the park. Some treasured time with my saxophone is up next, after which my teaching day begins. For me, this daily routine provides a perfect balance of music, nature and love, the three components I need to live and dream the life of the artist.

PART ONE:
THE PHYSICAL

PART ONE: THE PHYSICAL
QUALITY OF SOUND

Quality of sound is based on positioning, air delivery, and finger coordination. These three components of flute artistry must be united, otherwise your sound and pitch will suffer. While these concepts may seem to be very simple, their flawless execution is mandatory for you to reach your highest potential as an artist.

1

POSITION

The position of the body and of the flute are of great importance and often overlooked. Improper positioning will affect your ability to deliver your air into the instrument, and your quality of sound will suffer the consequences.

The following are the basic rules of positioning:

1) Flute secured against the bottom lip
2) Fingers relaxed and curved over the keys
3) Body forward and relaxed

In preparation for playing, follow this idea: sit or stand in a forward, relaxed position and then *bring the flute to your lip and secure it. Do not allow the flute to dictate your positioning.* While this may seem like a trivial thing to mention, I beg to differ. I have witnessed so many flute players with their head either glued to their neck or pushed so high in the air that they look like they are scanning the cosmos. The result of this is always the same: *bad quality of sound.* And so I say once again: sit or stand in a forward, relaxed position and then *bring the flute to your lip.* If you follow this simple idea, you will give yourself the best chance for success.

The proper angle of how to hold the flute while playing is an issue that is of constant debate in the flute community, unnecessarily so. For this, I defer to my colleague Michel Debost and his brilliant book, *The Simple Flute.* In his definitive examination of flute playing, Debost states over and over again to *play in a position that feels comfortable to you.* While this may seem simplistic and rather obvious, Debost points out that many flutists try to copy other players and how they hold their instrument, which often leads to disastrous results. And so I will agree with Debost and suggest you simply find an angle that is comfortable for you and stick with it.

The next idea is with regards to the *positioning of your left index finger.* This is unquestionably the most important finger you have for your flute playing.

It is the only finger that locks the flute into position on your lip by *pushing towards your right shoulder.* I advise my students to form the letter "C" with their left hand and to then pick up their flute. After that, make sure that your hand is turned inward so that your index finger rests solidly against the flute – do not allow it to float freely, unanchored, as most flutists do. *Your left index finger must push against the flute in order to secure its steady, solid placement against your bottom lip.* No matter what phrase or piece you come up against, you must never allow your left index finger to leave its position, or you will put your quality of sound at risk. I have witnessed countless beginners who do not have this finger in the correct position. Oftentimes, they will rest the flute against their left shoulder as an alternative - this is to be strictly avoided. Despite the fact that it may take longer for the student to be able to place the left index finger in its proper position, it is the only way to ensure that the flute remains stable and anchored, which is an absolute necessity in creating a steady, unbroken air delivery to the bell.

Another positioning idea that is usually overlooked is the *placement of the G and Ab fingers on the left hand.* Most young players are not taught to cover the G key with their fourth finger, so as a result, it is left dangling on the outer edge of the key. I remain puzzled as to why so many teachers do not demand their students position this finger properly. What I advise my students to do is to first place their left hand on the flute so that all the keys are perfectly covered and to then and only then bring the flute up to their lip, *without allowing their finger position to change.* This will ensure that their left arm position is correct, while not disrupting their finger position. It should also be noted that while the improper placement of the Ab and G finger will not cause significant problems for closed hole flutes, it will most definitely cause major problems for open hole ones. Most importantly, it will affect one's ability to have a smooth, secure technique when using the left hand. After all, we only have two hands and 10 fingers to work with!

Sticking with the Ab key, most beginners place this finger *underneath the flute* while playing, as a way to help hold the instrument. This often occurs because, as mentioned previously, the left index finger is improperly positioned. This is a disastrous scenario, and should be avoided at all costs. Instead, the Ab finger should rest *directly above the Ab key*, and not underneath it. This is imperative in order for the G finger to cover its key, as this finger works in conjunction with the Ab. Again, if your left index finger is correctly positioned, the flute will be secured without you having to hold on with your pinky. *Your thumbs should be the only two fingers that rest underneath the instrument.*

A further positioning idea with regards to your finger placement is as follows: make sure that both of your hands are *over top of the flute keyboard, and not underneath.* I have seen many students whose fingers are actually *underneath the flute,* which forces them to reach upwards to try and play the keys. This is a huge positioning error. Instead, form the letter "C" with both of your hands so your fingers descend upon the keys. This will give you the opportunity to master the open and closed fingering technique, which we will discuss in a later chapter.

A final idea re positioning is *the use of your body to play the flute.* I cannot tell you how many times I have experienced dizziness when watching a flute player's performance. Oftentimes the player is extraordinary, but the endless gyrations, waving back and forth (as though on a boat on a windy day) nullifies anything the player is presenting creatively. I have often wondered why flutists do this so often. Perhaps it is because the flute is so lightweight and easy to manipulate; perhaps they have been a dancer in a former life. Whatever the reason, this is an extremely bad approach, because it affects your air delivery into the flute, takes physical energy away from your fingers, and distracts the audience to no end. While I understand and appreciate that emotion plays a vital part in flute performance, the fact of the matter is that *all body moves make absolutely no difference to your quality of sound and should be reduced to a bare minimum.* Yes, play with emotion, but do not allow your body to participate in that emotion, *unless it is absolutely essential to your performance.*

I remember going to an outdoor concert in the 1980s at The Hollywood Bowl in Los Angeles, featuring the legendary flutist Jean-Pierre Rampal, accompanied only by his pianist. Despite the fact that it was a large outdoor venue, Rampal used no microphone, while he remained in a forward, relaxed, still position throughout the entire performance, his angelic sound filling the entire earth and sky, even all the way up to the cheap seats, where I, as a young student, was seated. Do not move your body when you play the flute – you are not a dancer, except with your fingers!

2

AIR

The invisible, mysterious, colorful airstream is the second physical component of flute artistry.

While there are many schools of thought regarding how to deliver the air into the flute, there are some fundamental ideas which I believe are extremely helpful in order to help you produce the most beautiful sound possible from your flute.

The first idea examines *how to send the air into the flute.* Lift your top teeth, take a deep, relaxed breath into your body, then allow your teeth to fall back down towards the mouthpiece, pushing the air from the deepest part of you into the deepest part of the flute. I call this idea "Bell to bell."

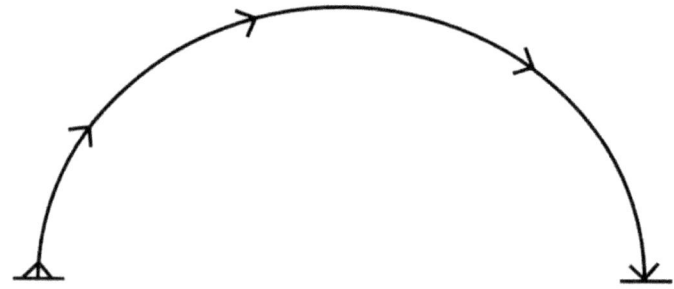

"Bell To Bell"
Air travels from the bell of our body to the bell of the flute

I often ask my students what their favorite color is and then ask them to close their eyes and see that color illuminating the inside of their flute when they play. I also ask them to choose something visual that creates an image of flowing, such as water, a beam of light, lava, or my personal favorite, the violin bow. By seeing the air in your mind's eye, you can better direct its delivery through the flute, which will give you the fullest, deepest sound and vibration in every note you play.

Another extremely important procedure re delivering the air is to *keep your bottom lip anchored against the head joint at all times.* When breathing, do not allow it to move in any way, shape or form as this will cause you to lose your spot and your air will go flying into outer space. Always keep your bottom lip secured against the head joint – this is crucial to maintaining your quality of sound.

NOTE: As previously discussed, the correct placement of the left index finger is the key to ensuring that the bottom lip stays anchored and in position when you play.

Taking your time when you breathe is also an important procedure to build into your air delivery. Instead of rushing your breaths, do the opposite and take a *full, deep breath* before beginning the next phrase. If you practice this technique of taking your time between breaths, you will be able to create the fullest and smoothest sound in your entrance notes. Many players jump at the first note after they breathe, creating a bad entrance and an accented sound (when one is not called for). Jumping at the first note can also create a forced, squeezed sound. While this kind of air delivery can sometimes be effective for loud, forceful passages, it is a disaster when attempting to play quietly. You must not interfere with the air on its journey into the flute, especially by any manipulation from your tongue or mouth.

NOTE: Most teachers advise their students to tongue every first note they play. This is a mistake, especially for the rank beginner, because it stops them from learning the legato stroke, the most important stroke in all playing. It also impedes the air from traveling freely into the flute without manipulation. Tonguing every single first note is a one-dimensional approach that limits the flutist in their style and nuance, and should be avoided, especially at the beginning of learning the flute. Once the legato stroke has been firmly established, then and only then should the tongue be introduced.

In order to start the air without the tongue, push the air through your body in a "V" shape, using the syllable "F" to deliver it. This will remove the tongue from the process and give you a smooth beginning to all of your entrance notes.

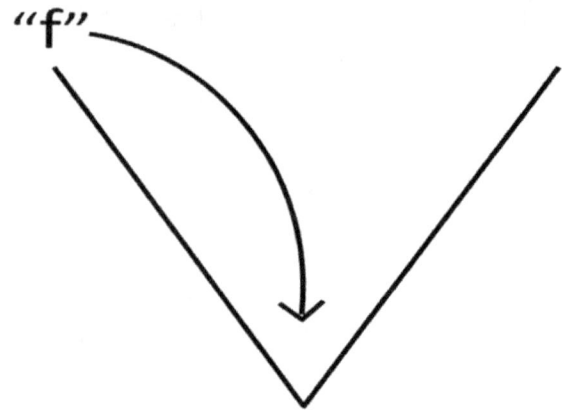

Air travels in a "V" shape to the bottom of the flute by saying "f" when we push the air into the horn

How much air to put into the flute also needs to be discussed. Because your airstream is invisible, it is difficult to measure how much energy you need to perfect each and every sound you create. We also have the problem of range on the flute. Unlike the piano, where every key has the same feel and vibration to it, the resonance and vibration of the low notes on the flute have a completely different feel to them than the higher ones. While the middle register of the instrument is fairly stable for most players, the high and low registers are the most uneven regarding air delivery. Unfortunately, most flute players try to solve this problem by overblowing, which creates an overbearing, unattractive sound.

In order to conquer this problem, start out by pushing *the same amount of air into every note. Do not pay any attention to dynamic markings.* Play with a conversational tone; not too loud, not too soft, but steady and warm. Try to match all of the sounds you create. Play slowly and carefully and let your air soak into every note you play. This "sameness of sound" you produce will be the foundation of your quality of sound and once established, will be where you build your dynamics from.

A further process to consider is *what type of sound* you should be sending into your flute. I always advise my students to work on producing an enticing, beautiful sound first. You must find the beauty in the sound – *your beauty.*

You are an *"earchitect;"* a master of the sound you create. Think of what is beautiful to you: a lover's smile, a colorful rose, an enchanting butterfly. Close your eyes, "see" this beauty and deliver it, through your airstream, into the flute. It is your job as a flutist and an artist to do so. Perfectly executing black notes on a white page accomplishes nothing except technique. It is only when you learn to open your inner ear and listen, *truly listen*, that you can create your own sound, a sound that will distinguish you from everybody else. This is the real secret to becoming an artist on the instrument: *the ability to hear, feel and deliver your beauty into the flute*, for all of us to vicariously feed off of. This individuality of sound is, in my opinion, the most important trait a flute player must have and surprisingly, the one that is most often overlooked.

Phil used to always tell me: "Once you get your sound, it's yours; some people might not like it, but it's yours and nobody can take it away from you." And of course, he was right.

NOTE: There are, without question, many other emotions and sounds that you must also learn to express in your playing, but I feel strongly that beauty is the first sound you should focus on, as its power and magnetism are nothing short of hypnotic to the listener.

A final idea examines *where to send your air into the flute.* Again, the use of imagery is a highly valuable tool for you to use. Imagine a spot at the end of the flute where your air goes. Every time you take a breath and begin the next phrase, send your air to that *exact same spot,* regardless of whether it is a high note or a low note. I oftentimes ask my students to imagine there is a candle flame at the end of their flute and ask them to "blow it out" on every entrance they make. I also ask them to imagine they are dropping a coin into a wishing well and instruct them to let the coin drop as long as possible before they hear it splash in the water. A third idea I present to my students with regards to airflow is the bathtub. I ask them to go home, turn on the bathtub spout and watch what occurs. Despite the curious looks I receive from my students, the bathtub idea works because it creates a perfect visual picture of where our air should travel when we play – downwards, forever flowing, aided and directed by the powerful force of gravity.

Because your air is invisible, you must create a picture of it in your mind and ear. Unlike violinists, for example, who can see every move they make with their bow and fingers, you are blind – *you cannot see your air or your fingers.* As a result, most flutists simply blow into the instrument with no concept of directing it whatsoever. However, if you can learn to visualize your airstream and execute its delivery to the bottom of the flute, you can discover the true sound of the instrument, a sound that is incredibly beautiful in its color, depth, and pitch.

3

FINGERS

The fingers, the third physical component of flute artistry, are often overlooked. From a positioning perspective, it is vital that the fingers are curved over the keys. I ask my students to curl their hands like the letter "C" and then place their fingers on the keys. The fingers should move up and down like a spring, *from the knuckles only*. Ideally, your fingers *should never leave the keys.*

This finger technique requires great patience and dedication to master and only the flutist who can acquire this finger positioning will be able to surmount the many difficult technical passages he or she will come up against. It is still baffling to me, after teaching the flute for almost 40 years, how many flutists (many of them quite accomplished) have come into my room displaying a haphazard approach to the placement of their fingers on the instrument. They bang up and down on the keys with the middle part of their fingers, as opposed to carefully opening and closing the keys with the round part of their fingertips.

This problem occurs because the player has not been taught properly from the outset and has developed this "slapping up and down" technique, which is disastrous when trying to execute both speed and centered sound production. You must also not allow the fingers on the left hand to play on the edge of the keys, but instead curve your hand sufficiently in order to ensure correct placement of the fingers on the keys. *Your fingers phrase for you* and must be in the best position possible in order for you to be successful.

A story from legendary jazz alto saxophonist Sonny Criss perfectly illustrates the value of finger positioning. When Sonny was just 19 years old, he had the incredible fortune to play beside his idol, Charlie Parker. After Sonny listened to Bird play one amazing solo after another, he summoned up his courage and asked the great master, "Goddammit, Bird, how do you do it?" Then Sonny recounted, "Bird didn't say nothin' to me boy, but the next time he took a solo he turned around and played right in my face! It's all fingers, boy! *It's all fingers!"*

OPEN VS. CLOSED

The flute is based on the open and closed fingering system. A closed note is when you put your fingers down (eg., A to G), whereas an open note is when you pick your fingers up (e.g, G to A). This opposite movement presents the problem of gravity vs. antigravity in our fingering. Unlike pianists, who use gravity in closing every note they play, we are constantly moving in two different directions with our fingers. This makes playing in tune extremely difficult. In fact, the problem of matching the open vs. closed moves on the flute is the *fundamental reason for all pitch problems on the instrument.*

In order to overcome this problem, you must first teach your fingers to stay *as close to the keys as possible.* When closing, put your fingers down firmly and avoid any banging or hitting. When opening, lift your fingers up slowly and carefully to prevent your fingers from leaving the keys. Your fingers should caress the keys as you would when caressing your lover – with the gentlest, subtlest touch possible.

NOTE: There are some moves on the flute where you are closing and opening at the same time, for example, Bb to B or F to Gb. In these cases, always treat the move as an open one because of the difficulty in executing it cleanly. There are also times when you close with your finger but the key actually opens, such as D to Eb or G to Ab. In these cases, treat the move as a closed one and execute it firmly, without attacking the key.

During my time with Phil, I remember him telling me, "It doesn't matter whether you know the names of the notes or not – all that matters is whether you know if you are opening or closing."

This is a brilliant observation, because it makes reading the notes secondary to mastering the opening and closing of your fingers. Simply stated, without a seamless transition between your open and closed fingering, you have no chance to play the flute in tune, as your airstream will be continuously rerouted and disrupted from its journey into the instrument.

NOTE: When executing open and closed correctly, your sound will become quieter and flatter to your ear but will actually be the correct pitch of the flute.

PART TWO:

TECHNIQUE

PART TWO:

TECHNIQUE

The word "technique" is a misunderstood one for flutists and musicians in general. Technique is not the ability to play scales and patterns perfectly with a metronome; it is the ability to play any exercise or piece with *intonation, rhythm, and your own quality of sound.* The ideas presented in this section will endeavour to help you achieve exactly that.

4

THE FOUR CORNERSTONES

The four cornerstones present four different ways to tackle any exercise or song in your repertoire. By carefully examining each of these cornerstones, you can take apart any piece to produce the best quality of sound possible in your flute. While this approach requires playing the piece four separate times, the benefits of doing so far outweigh the work involved. The old saying "Talent is 1% inspiration and 99% perspiration" applies here. Upon completion, you will be thoroughly informed as to the inner workings of the piece, and that knowledge will serve as the foundation for when you add the final ingredient, interpretation.

The success of the four cornerstones approach is predicated on one simple idea: *do not use any tempo whatsoever in your study.* Tempo will be the *last ingredient* you add to your playing, not the first. Throw your metronome away and discover the art of listening; there can be no greater benefit for you. Once the four cornerstones are solidified in your mind, ear and finger, you can then add the tempo, but not before.

Actors, dancers, athletes and many other creative people often start by *slowing the creative process down* so they can absorb and perfect the particular moves needed to master the piece they are creating. The final tempo is only added at the end. For some reason I have never understood, musicians rarely do this, instead playing everything from the get-go in the final tempo. In my opinion this is a mistake, because it does not allow you the opportunity to take the piece apart, thoroughly examine it, and then put it back together. However if you begin with the four cornerstones approach, you will be able to do exactly that, and in the process, thoroughly decipher and master every piece you play.

NOTE: For all of the four cornerstones, a simple line drawn over a chosen note of importance is highly recommended, so you can easily identify the crucial notes of your phrases.

THE ENTRANCE NOTE

The entrance note is the first process of the four cornerstones. The entrance note occurs *every time you take a breath and begin a phrase.* Deliver the entrance note to the bottom of the flute, *without tempo.* Listen for a warm, full sound and visualize its journey through the flute. The longer you allow the entrance note to play, the better, because that length will eliminate tempo and allow your ear to become responsible for the production of your sound. Allow your entrance notes to fill up the flute in the same way as when you pour yourself a glass of water — *from the bottom to the top.*

When you feel the entrance note has reached the bell of the flute, continue that same sound throughout the remaining notes in the phrase until your next breath. Then repeat the process of listening to the entrance note in each and every phrase you begin thereafter.

NOTE: The standard approach when playing a piece is to look at the metronomic marking and then play the piece in that tempo. By abandoning that and luxuriating and listening to all of your entrance notes, you are *setting the tone* for all of your phrases. As mentioned previously, you are an "earchitect" of sound. Your ear must be *completely engaged and be the most important part of your playing.* Without it, you will play as if deaf. Music is not about reading and counting; it is about *listening and feeling.* The sound of your entrance notes should be your *number one priority.* If you do not listen to your entrance notes you will only have tempo in your playing, and that will not be enough to develop the fullest, deepest sound in your flute, nor will it be enough to make the listener feel anything. It goes without saying that even the most virtuosic technical performance is worthless if it does not move the listener. Phil would always tell me, "If your first note isn't right, your second and third notes won't be right either; you have to grab people right away, or they will turn off."

Imagine a lightbulb. Every time you turn it on, the light races into it, but when it is turned off, the light instantly disappears. The same holds true for your flute. When you play, you illuminate it; when you stop, the flute goes dark. A lightbulb has no variables; the light goes into the bulb with the same intensity every time, but when you "turn the light on" in your flute, *you are responsible* for delivering the right amount of energy into every entrance note you create. This is a major key in establishing your own quality of sound; the ability to start every phrase with the sound *you* like, according to your ear.

I always encourage my students to study the sound of their entrance notes with their *eyes closed.* When the eyes close, the ears open and there is no visual distraction to interfere with the listening process.

Ex. of entrance notes on "Early Autumn"

THE BOTTOM NOTE

The bottom note is the second process of the four cornerstones. The bottom note occurs every time you reach the *lowest note of a phrase*. Whenever you reach this note, you must play it *without tempo and for as long as possible*. The purpose of doing this is so that you do not cut off the bottom vibration of your sound and phrases, which is of vital importance in creating a warm, tuned sound on your flute.

Interestingly, when reading music, the human eye sees things vertically and not horizontally. Because of this, the high notes get most, if not all of the attention, while the bottom notes are ignored altogether. In order to overcome this, you need to be a detective and train your eye to *search out and illuminate every bottom note you find*. By doing this, you will be amazed at how much richer and fuller your flute sounds.

Ex. of bottom notes on "Body Heat"

Phil would say, "There are two kinds of players: top note players, and bottom note players. Top note players miss many important notes, but bottom note players see *everything*." Once I became aware of this, I realized I had been a top note player my whole life and immediately changed my approach, with startling results. Become a bottom note player and revolutionize your quality of sound!

NOTE: Sometimes in a musical phrase there will be a succession of bottom notes. When that occurs, stretch and color *the last bottom note of the group only.*

Ex. of succession of bottom notes

Another critical reason to find and listen to all bottom notes is because most of the time, the bottom note is closed and the note after it is open. In order to control the sound of the open note, you must give yourself as much time as possible to execute a perfect finger move or your airstream will change direction and the pitch of your flute will suffer. *Always play the bottom note for as long as possible!*

Imagine a roller coaster. At first, you climb up to its highest peak and then you hurtle downwards to its lowest spot, only to repeat this process for the duration of the ride. And so it is the same for the flutist when reading a musical phrase. Every time you reach the lowest note of the phrase, *settle the sound in the bottom of the flute.*

NOTE: This technique is not exclusive to flute playing and can greatly enhance the sound of any other instrumentalist or vocalist. It is an idea, a style of playing that aims to deliver the deepest sound possible into your instrument, *from the bottom up.* Again, because everyone has been taught to play in tempo, they have never had a chance to experiment with time or the length of notes and therefore have never developed any kind of sound or style in their playing. Identifying and listening to all of your bottom notes is a process, an examination. Think like a scientist, with curiosity and interest. Afterwards, you can add the final ingredient to your phrases, interpretation, of which tempo is a part of, but even then, you must still honor and recognize the bottom notes and color them as much as possible. As the saying goes, "Life is like a lemon; squeeze the most out of it that you can." And with regards to this key element of flute playing, I offer the following idea: when you play and listen to your bottom notes, *visualize in your mind a long, dark corridor in which your bottom notes fall down and into.*

LONG TO SHORT

Long to short is the third cornerstone of flute artistry. Every time you play a long note followed by a short note or a series of short notes, *take the first short note and stretch its length for as long as possible, without tempo.* The purpose of doing this is to *connect the first short note to the bottom of the flute* to give it a rich and full quality of sound. This technique will also stop you from crowding the short notes together, which automatically happens when you play in tempo. Again, the human eye is at fault here. Attracted to the long note, it holds onto it for too long and then moves over at the last second to play the group of short notes. The result of this is that the flutist comes in late, jamming all the short notes together, killing the rhythm and motion of the phrase while deadening the vibration of the horn. As soon as you play the long note, *immediately move your eye over to the first short note in preparation for its entrance.* This will eliminate the "holding sound" in your long notes, something all players suffer from. You must learn to, like a violinist, bow through the long note while preparing your move to the first short note. This allows the long note to be free and full of motion. You can play the long note as long as you want to, as long as you are looking at the short note that is upcoming. This is a vital key to the success of this idea and phrasing, in general. *Never hold the long note – always release it to the short note.*

Despite the fact that long to short exists everywhere in music, most players have no concept of it and have never seen it. Oftentimes you will discover that the first short note is also a bottom note, which gives you two reasons to lengthen it. Sometimes it will be an entrance note as well. In the same way that the great artist Michelangelo started his sculpture with a huge piece of marble and then methodically chipped away at it, you too must start with a huge first short note. After carefully perfecting the sound of it and its connection to the previous long note, you can then begin to "chip away" at the length of the note until it becomes exactly the right length that you need. As Phil told me countless times, *"Never play a skinny first short note!"*

Ex. of long to short on "Beethoven's 9th"

The dotted eighth to sixteenth note rhythm (the staple of swing music) is a perfect study of long to short moves. As soon as you play the dotted eighth, move over to the sixteenth and introduce it as early as possible. Most players hold the dotted eighth and arrive at the sixteenth late, which disrupts the motion of the swing rhythm. Your job is to *move to the short note as soon as possible,* in order to create a free sound that has motion in it. Count Basie's sax section did this to perfection, creating what became known as "The Basie Sound," a flawless motion they created between the long to short moves inherent in the swing rhythm.

Ex. of swing rhythm and inherent long to short on "Oh, You Crazy Moon"

The final, extremely important idea re long to short concerns breathing. Many flutists pick the wrong spot to take a breath, and in doing so, disrupt their phrasing and quality of sound. Begin with the process of taking a breath between *every long note and short note.* This is the perfect place to breathe because it gives you time to let the long note go, take a full, deep breath, and then introduce the first short note. Remember to avoid tempo when practicing this procedure. Once you have mastered this technique you will have to decide, based on the story you are telling, which long to short moves to breathe between. Obviously, when you are playing a song that has lyrics, you will use those lyrics to guide you, but when the piece is an instrumental one, I advise the following: *always start by breathing between every long to short move.*

Ex. of long to short breathing on "Indiscreet"

OPEN VS. CLOSED

The fourth and final process of the four cornerstones is the study of open vs. closed finger moves. As previously mentioned, the open move occurs whenever you pick your fingers up (e.g. G to A), while the closed move occurs whenever you put your fingers down (e.g. A to G). It is of paramount importance that you meticulously examine the open vs. closed moves in every piece you play, because it is your step by step guide to exactly what direction your fingers are moving. This is by far the most grueling part of the four cornerstones study because it requires that you examine *every single finger move you make.*

Once you recognize every open and closed move, you can then develop the touch necessary to execute these opposite moves without disturbing your airstream. Again, playing in tempo creates a major problem, as it forces your fingers to react before they are oftentimes ready to, which results in slamming down the closed keys while flying off the open ones.

Because of this, you should play every closed and open move on the piece you are studying *slowly and carefully.* As the closed note uses gravity, stretch its length and allow it to sink into the flute as deeply as possible. When you move to the open note, finger it with *no emphasis whatsoever.* This will help you match the gravity to anti-gravity moves the open and closed fingering system presents. Any attention paid to the open note will result in it being overplayed, and your flute will lose its pitch and bottom sound. *Always give to the closed and take away from the open.*

Ex. of "closed vs. open"
Give to the closed Bb with no emphasis on the open C

NOTE: There are a few exceptions to not emphasizing open notes. If it is an entrance note, bottom note, or the first short note after a long note, it must be stretched and colored without exception. If the open note is an important note to the melody, it must also be emphasized. Still, even if the open note is a vital sound in the story, the move to it must be as perfectly timed as possible or it will lose its center and bell sound.

An excellent way to study the open and closed moves is to visualize the bow of the violin, as it moves back and forth, horizontally, across the strings. "Bow" each note as long as possible and make each note an independent move by bowing the closed note in one direction and the open note in the other. This will ensure that every note has its own life and length and will eliminate all "combinations" in your moves, so that every sound you produce is its own, like a series of beads joined together, one by one, by a string that goes through each and every one of them. The open and closed moves must be strung individually to ensure the pitch is correct, while the uninterrupted airstream is the "string" that connects them all together.

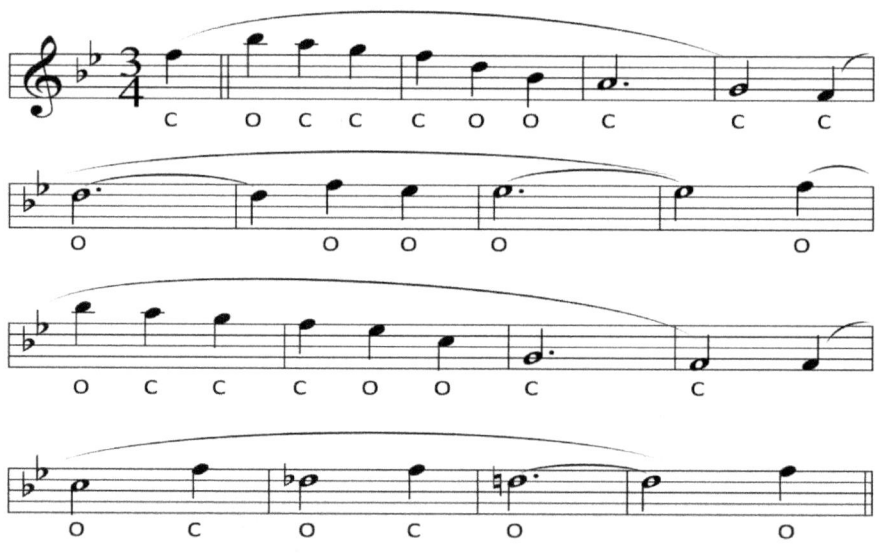

Ex. of closed vs. open on "Charmaine"

Another interesting aspect of open vs. closed is that most of the notes of the flute can be both closed or opened. Take the note G, for example. When you move from F to G, you open the G, but when you move from A to G, you close it. It is imperative that whether you are opening or closing you produce the *same sound in the note*, or else you will produce two different sounds for every note you play, which will ruin your intonation and your ability to blend with other instruments.

Clearly, there are some closed to open moves that are much more difficult than others (such as D to Db, for example) but if you practice carefully, slowly and horizontally, you will eventually match all of the sounds in your playing, regardless of the direction your fingers are moving. *This is where true pitch and intonation comes from.* Tuning up to a single note is utterly worthless if you make faulty open and closed finger moves. You must learn to tune all of your notes on the flute with your ear and not rely on anything else. This is the essence of the four cornerstones approach: *to make you responsible, through dedicated work and listening, for every sound you create.*

NOTE: When working on the four cornerstones, *play everything as smoothly as possible.* Only use the tongue when you see repeated notes. This will allow you to focus all of your attention on mastering the sound of your flute, *before adding the articulations the piece requires.*

change to:

then back to:

5

ARTICULATION

Articulation, or how we speak on the flute, is a fascinating subject to examine. The flutist has only two articulation options available: tonguing or non-tonguing. Unfortunately, most flutists are taught to start with tonguing, which presents a myriad of problems for the beginner. It forces the mouth to become involved in starting every phrase; it makes it much more difficult to develop intonation and send the air through the flute to the bell; and it can cause the entrance notes to be accented and choppy sounding. For these reasons, I do not introduce tonguing until the student can first produce a smooth, uninterrupted legato sound in their playing.

LEGATO PLAYING

The first rule of legato (non-tongued) playing is to *never let the sound stop.* Deliver the air to the bottom of the flute and maintain that airflow *throughout the phrase.* The flawless execution of your open and closed fingering is also mandatory for your phrasing to be unbroken. Many players have "holes" between their finger moves, when the airstream suddenly stops for a moment – a disaster when playing legato. Phil used to tell me, "When you play, you are two people: an air machine and a finger machine." This combination of a flowing airstream with perfectly synchronized finger moves creates the pure legato sound, which I believe is the most important component of flute artistry.

NOTE: In order to play in this manner, you will need to select pieces that have no repeated notes. There are several exercises and songs that will provide this option for you.

Ex. of legato playing on "When I Lost You"

The second rule of legato playing is to *close the first note of the piece.* If the first note is a G, for example, start with your fingers on A. When you put the air into the flute, close the G key at the same time so that *the air meets the finger at the key.* This will allow you to use gravity to ensure the air flows downwards and will eliminate your mouth from the process.

NOTE: Most flute players start every phrase by tonguing the first note, without moving a finger. This should be strictly avoided in legato playing. Your mouth's role should be to stay firm, in position, and to act as a conduit for the air to travel through.

Start on the "A"

Ex. of closing the first note of the piece on Mozart's "Eine Kleine Nachtmusik"

The third rule of legato playing is to *"freeze" your fingers when taking a breath between phrases.* If the last note of the phrase is a G, for example, leave your fingers on the G and *do not move to the next note until you begin your air.*

Freezing your fingers allows your air and finger to start the next note *together*. Freezing also enables you to determine whether the upcoming note is open or closed, bottom or top, etc., which helps you to better "see" how and where your fingers are moving when you start your phrases.

NOTE: Sometimes when you freeze your fingers between breaths, the note after the breath is the same as the one you are frozen on. When that is the case, *simply lift up one finger* so that you can use gravity to close the first note of the new phrase.

Ex. of freezing fingers between breaths on "Sophisticated Lady"

TONGUING

Once you have mastered the legato sound, the second part of articulation, *tonguing*, can be introduced. The first step in my approach to tonguing is to *never tongue the first note of any phrase*. Use your air and finger only to begin the phrase, exactly as you do when playing legato, as this will allow the first note to fall into the flute before you begin tonguing the rest of the notes. This is essential to protect the intonation of your instrument, which should always be your number one priority, regardless of what type of articulation you have decided upon.

There are two basic types of tonguing: the legato or "dah" type and the staccato or "tah" type. Both of these need to be mastered so that the flutist can move between each type with ease.

The legato or "dah" stroke hits the roof of the mouth and is used for a smooth attack, while the staccato or "tah" attack hits the back of the top teeth and is used for a sharp, pointed attack. Take any series of notes that are repeated and practice both types of tonguing, slowly at first and then add more speed as your tongue gets more agile. Think of the tongue as a hammer hitting a nail – it strikes quickly, pulls back, then strikes again. This approach will give you a clean, precise beginning to your tongued notes.

Double and triple tonguing are also components of flute artistry. The T and K syllables are best for staccato passages, while the D and G syllables are more effective for slower ones. Practice both options, *slowly at first*, gradually increasing the speed as your tongue becomes more supple with this tonguing technique.

Adding the tongue to your playing dictates that there are now three things that have to be coordinated to execute the sound of the note: the air, the finger, and the tongue. Many players sound completely different when they play smoothly as opposed to when they tongue. For this reason, I first present a phrase to my students that has no repeated notes and ask them to play through it smoothly. After that, I ask them to play the same phrase again but this time with the tongue. In this way they can work on matching the sound between legato and tonguing, which is vital to ensuring your quality of sound is not altered in any way by the articulation you are using.

Ex. of legato phrase / then tongued phrase to match sound

NOTE: Many pieces of music have little or no articulation markings or incorrect ones. Because of this, it is essential that you do not simply follow what is on the page, but instead, *make your own decisions about how you want to articulate every phrase of every piece.* It is your job, as an artist, to do so, and is a major part of interpretation, which will be discussed in a later chapter. By making your own decisions regarding articulation, you will distinguish yourself from the herd of readers who adhere only to the written instructions on the page. And with regards to your choice of articulation, I offer the following idea: *Always play the flute as smoothly and connectedly as possible, even when using the tongue.*

6

DYNAMICS

Dynamics, "the science of strength," is an underrated and undervalued component of flute artistry. It is of paramount importance that you determine the dynamic of *every finger move and phrase you play*. Most players simply follow the markings on the page and many seem oblivious even to those, deciding instead to play everything they see as loudly as possible. This bombastic approach to playing in today's world has become so prevalent that dynamics have almost become a lost art. This is a huge mistake on the part of the musical community, because it makes music one-dimensional and eliminates subtlety and nuance. It is no accomplishment to play this way; rather, it reveals a total lack of sensitivity and artistry. A flute player should be like a chameleon, changing colors constantly to display and reveal the intricate nuances of the piece at hand. Simply blowing loudly with no dynamic shading whatsoever reeks of amateurism and should be avoided.

What I advise my students is to first observe the dynamics as written and then to make *their own decisions as to the dynamics needed* for the telling of the story. This also requires that you thoroughly understand the composition at hand and the climaxes of the piece, so that you can build your dynamics towards them. If you use your common sense, understand the piece, and follow your heart, you cannot go wrong.

NOTE: Pay special attention to not allow your dynamics to change between your open and closed finger moves. Opening too quickly will make the flute suddenly louder; closing too abruptly will deaden the sound. You must be a master of your finger changes, or you will never be able to fully control your dynamic shading and nuance.

Despite the fact that dynamics have been seemingly tossed aside in this day and age, there are many great artists who have used them to enhance their performances and compositions. This is the power of dynamics, the wonderful opportunity to explore the limitless possibilities of color and nuance your flute can produce, your only obligation being to serve the melody. And with regards to this vital part of flute performance, I offer the following advice: despite the volume you are using, *always try to present the warmth and beauty of your sound in your dynamic shading.*

7
ACCENTS

Accents, the sudden change of volume and intensity of sound, are exceedingly important to flute playing. Without them, music is nothing short of monotonous.

There are two basic types of accents at our disposal: the "hat," where the note is attacked with great ferocity and then cut off abruptly, and the "legato accent," where the accent is of a longer, more stable duration. As with all reading, your approach should be to follow the accents on the page and then experiment with your own ideas.

The unparalleled master of the accent and its use was Ludwig Van Beethoven. He spared no detail in ensuring that the accents he required in his music were explicitly noted on the page. Listen to any of Beethoven's compositions while reading the score and observe his use of accents. Undoubtedly, he knew the value of them and used them constantly through his stunning compositions.

When you are working on accenting a piece, let your natural emotions tell you when to accent or "lean on" a note or series of notes. *Any heightening of a note is an accent.* It can be soft and exquisite like a lover's touch, or powerful and forceful like a bull goring a matador. It is up to you, the artist, to determine the *exact strength and nature of the accent.*

Unfortunately, because of bad training and mouth playing, many flutists accent when they do not intend to. Other players accent so frequently that the accent loses its intrinsic value, which is to suddenly heighten a note or series of notes. While there is no one steadfast rule regarding accents, you should always use the story of the piece you are playing as your guide to their use. As an exercise, I often ask my students to accent something they do not think should be accented, to reveal to them how improper accenting destroys the musical phrase. Accents are like seasoning on a meal: too much will destroy the taste, while just enough will complement the flavor of the cuisine.

My first and greatest lesson regarding accents came from listening to the Count Basie band at a live concert in 1976. The first song of the evening started at a nice pace with a very relaxed, smooth swing feel that typified the "Basie sound." Just as the audience was settling into the groove of the song, the band suddenly accented a single quarter note with the greatest intensity imaginable. The entire audience shrieked with terror and jumped out of their seats, followed by relief and peals of laughter as the band returned to its initial, relaxed sound. This was my introduction to the power of accents and it left a deep impression on me.

8

VIBRATO

The use of vibrato is a vital ingredient in flute artistry. It is described as a "rapid, slight variation of pitch" and when expertly used, adds a beautiful nuance to your playing. Unfortunately, it can also destroy your quality of sound and make you unbearable to listen to. Vibrato is an extremely disciplined procedure and in order to master it you must be willing to put in many hours of painstaking work.

The first step of vibrato training is to start by using *your jaw only*. Deliver the air of the first note to the bottom of the flute, and then move your jaw, slowly and methodically, saying the syllable "wah." Do eight vibrations for each note of the exercise, followed by six and then four. Do not try to make the vibrations sound pretty but instead, focus on making them sound *mechanical only*. Make sure you can hear each and every one of the vibrations cleanly and clearly, and practice as slowly as possible.

8/6/4 vibrations and breathe after every note

After you have mastered the above, the second step of vibrato training is *to increase the speed of the vibrations*. Once again, ensure that the note you are vibrating first travels *all the way through to the end of the flute* and then begin the vibrations at eight, six and four each. As you increase the speed, continue to demand clear and distinct vibrations. If the speed you are trying does not produce that, reduce the speed. As you practice this over and over, you will eventually be able to vibrate the notes with great rapidity.

NOTE: During this study you will discover that some of the notes on the flute are easier to vibrate than others. In general, the bottom notes on the flute present the most difficulty. Exercise patience in this area of the instrument and remember that the most important part of your vibrato training at this stage is to *cleanly and distinctly hear every single vibration of the note you are playing.*

The third and final stage of the vibrato process is to *"let the vibrato go."* Deliver the note to the bottom of the flute and then let the note vibrate naturally. Imagine it as a tornado, rapidly circling and vibrating inside your airstream. Use your ear to guide you as to the correct speed. Study and listen to the great artists and how they vibrato. Jascha Heifetz, Frank Sinatra and Sonny Criss instantly come to mind. Your vibrato can be influenced by others but should be your own. And with regards to this most beautiful addition to your quality of sound, I advise the following: use the vibrato sparingly, only on sustained notes, and *never start the vibrato until your air has settled into the bottom of the flute.*

On a personal note, my vibrato study with Phil lasted for six months and was a torturous time for me. I worked on it for six hours a day, seven days a week, and was not allowed to partake in anything else musical. Looking back, I would have to say that although it was the toughest part of my training, it was definitely worth it, as I was able to develop a disciplined yet flexible vibrato that was my own. I owe Phil a great debt for his steadfast insistence that I put all of my attention on my vibrato training until I had mastered its use. This was definitely the key to my overcoming this most difficult part of flute artistry.

NOTE: You will need to have many different speeds of your vibrato available to you, due to the many different emotions music creates. A tender love song, as an example, will need a gentle vibrato speed, whereas a driving rock song will demand another. This is the reason you must be in *complete control* *of the speed of the vibrations you produce.* Your vibrato must be flexible, and not fixed. *You must control the vibrato and not have it control you.* Most flutists and in particular, classical flutists, overdo their vibrato, using it far too often, while presenting it with one speed and one speed only. This approach is extremely taxing on the ear and should be avoided. The vibrato should be a lovely addition to your sound but should never upstage it. Think of a hearty bowl of soup as your quality of sound and your vibrato as the delicate seasoning that enhances its flavor, or a woman's sensual lips and the tiny bit of color she adds to them to make them even more alluring. This is your job, as an artist – to create the perfect speed and amount of vibrato, added at the perfect moments during the piece you are playing.

Another reason your vibrato speed must be flexible is when you are playing in an orchestra or wind ensemble. If you are playing the lead part, you must set the vibrato speed for the ensemble; if you are accompanying the lead, you must match the speed the lead player presents, *even if it is the wrong speed.* This is the key to the ensemble sounding as one, an art form that is basically lost in today's playing. Instead of playing as a group with the identical vibrato speed, the groups of today consist of individuals who use their own speeds, with no consideration for the other players around them.

This is very unfortunate and destroys the potential for the ensemble to sound as one. It also reflects how few flutists learn to truly master their vibrato; not only are they unwilling to match their vibrato speed to the lead player, *they are unable to.* This inability displays amateurism, insufficient training and lack of understanding. Master your vibrato; do not let it master you.

9

HORIZONTAL VS. VERTICAL

As previously mentioned, the human eye sees things vertically. High notes stick out like a sore thumb, while low notes are hidden and disregarded. Because of this, it is extremely important to train your eye to play every note horizontally, regardless of where it is on the written page.

Imagine you are playing the violin. Take any series of notes and "bow" each one separately and horizontally. See the bow moving across the strings, back and forth, as you play. Let each note bow as long as possible and when you change to the next note, *change direction with your bow stroke*. Play slowly and work on matching the sound of each and every note to its neighbor.

Ex. of bowing each note horizontally on F major scale

Phil would instruct me, "All the notes in music are on a horizontal line – there are no high or low notes, just horizontal ones." This is an extremely beneficial idea to add to your playing because it will stop you from "reaching" for high notes and overplaying them, as most flutists do. Again I refer to my colleague Debost and his brilliant idea that all high notes should be played from the bottom of your feet! If you can see every note horizontally, you will keep the air flowing into the bell and, in doing so, match their sounds with greater expertise. Remember to take your time between your horizontal moves and to play each note for as long as possible. After much work on this study, you will start to hear all of your notes settling into the flute, which will give all of them, even the highest ones you play, the deepest depth and color imaginable.

Ex. of horizontal playing on "Brahms' 4th"

After I left Phil's study, I continued to analyze his methods and ideas. One afternoon, while sweeping the floor with a broom, I suddenly had an epiphany that the sweeping back and forth motion was a perfect analogy for horizontal playing. I immediately raced to the phone to call Phil and inform him of my discovery, of which he was very impressed and congratulatory. A couple of weeks later, during our regular weekly phone call, Phil suddenly announced, "I've got a great new idea for you to work on; it's called sweeping!" Pretending that I had not told him this very idea just a few weeks before, I applauded him, while at the same time, had a little chuckle to myself.

10

TEMPO VS. RHYTHM

Tempo and rhythm are, in fact, the opposite of each other. Tempo implies playing at an unbending, robotic, metronomic pace. Rhythmic playing is like a series of waves at the ocean, all different shapes and speeds. Tempo is mechanical; rhythm is elastic, personal, heartfelt.

The use of tempo in teaching and performing is completely misunderstood. Tempo should serve as a guide only, giving you a general idea of the speed of the piece. That "guide" should be flexible however, based on your abilities as a performer and your inherent feeling of what speed you think works best *for you.* The academic world (particularly in classical music) is an example of the bland uniformity tempo playing reveals. It makes absolutely no sense to have thousands of flutists around the world playing the same pieces at the same tempos. This approach is totally uncreative and reeks of a lack of individuality, a trait every artist must have in order to be successful. Find your own speeds and rhythms, and be flexible; rigidity and conformity are non-artistic and destructive to your art.

I always tell my students that playing in tempo is like speaking in tempo, or eating in tempo - it results in monotony. Can you imagine a school full of students, sitting down in the cafeteria at lunch time, with a gigantic metronome dictating the tempo they are supposed to eat at? It sounds ridiculous but that is how musicians are taught to play music. Avoid tempo and instead, seek out the rhythmic pulses of your phrases. Every phrase is an individual one and should be treated as such. In fact, I will go so far as to say that *every single finger move you make should have its own rhythmic identity.*

Don't be a counting machine; *feel the music and the phrases, from your heart out*; otherwise, you will produce bland music that will not hold the listener's attention. From my perspective, there can be nothing worse. Beethoven said, "To play a wrong note is insignificant; to play without passion is inexcusable!" Tempo kills the passion in the music, while rhythm reveals it. Never forget this extremely important part of flute artistry!

Frank Sinatra, known around the world as "The Voice," used rhythmic phrasing to perfection when he sang. He left behind countless examples of his expertise in this regard. While the orchestra would lay down the basic groove of the song, Sinatra would float around the time, delivering his phrases in perfect rhythm, while always, first and foremost, *serving the melody.* His ability to do this was uncanny and separated him from all the other singers of his time. This is the real secret to phrasing: the ability to transcend tempo, while phrasing rhythmically, based on the story you are telling. Throw your metronome away, feel the inherent rhythms of the music and don't just read — *SING!*

11

COLOR & CIRCLE / PLANT & FLOWER

These two concepts aim to help you identify the important notes in your phrases, while moving through the others without emphasis. While these ideas may seem simple, they are designed to give you a couple of different ways to think about phrasing and motion.

Color and circle: Think of every note as a *complete circle.* Every time you play a note, visualize it starting at *the bottom of the circle.* Whenever you arrive at an important note, let it sit longer at that spot before moving to the next note. As you control the speed of every note you play, your circles can all be different lengths but are connected to each other by your airstream. Whether the note is a high one or a low one, *always start every note at the bottom of the circle.* This will keep your air inside your instrument, stop you from "reaching" for the high notes, and help you play every note as deeply as possible. "Color notes" include all of your entrances, bottom notes, first short notes after a long note, closed notes, and any other notes you deem important. *The longer you color a note, the more important it becomes.* Stretch the color notes and move all the other connecting notes with the unending circle. Phil used to call this *"playing in the oval."*

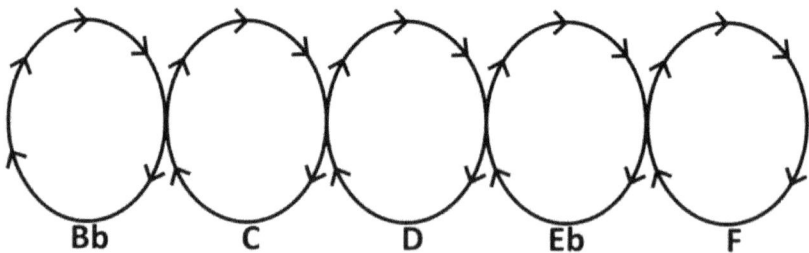

| Bb | C | D | Eb | F |

Plant and flower: Have you ever planted anything? A flower, a tomato plant, a tree? You first dig a hole into the earth, place the seeds or the plant in the ground, firm the earth back up, and then water. If you do not plant the seeds or the plant correctly, the plant will not flourish. This same process can be thought of when you play your flute. "Plant" all the important notes into the ground, "seed" them deeply and fully into the bell, and the notes born thereafter will be the "flowers." I often think of a rose and the struggle it goes through, winding its way further and further up, with thorns abundant, until its mesmerizing beauty is finally revealed. And so it is with the flutist, planting the color notes deeply into the ground, resulting in the rest of the notes flowering, *rooted from the bottom up*.

Ex. of plant and flower on Ab Major Scale

12

OCTAVE TO OCTAVE MOVES

Octave to octave moves present an interesting challenge for the flute player. Because of the human eye, the higher octave is always seen as more important than the lower one and winds up being overplayed in the extreme. When this happens, the quality of sound instantly leaves the bottom of the flute, where it heads off into outer space, to the galaxies beyond.

In order to solve this problem, put all of your attention on the bottom octave and color it *for as long as possible, without exception.* When you move to the higher octave, attach no emphasis to it whatsoever and make a gentle transition to the note. Because the flute is a free-blowing instrument with no resistance, you must be delicate in how you deliver the air to the higher octave. The slightest extra help or push will result in the note being too big for its purpose. Remember that violins and pianos play lighter and softer the higher they go, as they have no choice in the matter, since their strings are shorter at the top. Flute players would indeed be wise to emulate this idea and *always think lighter when playing the higher octave notes.* If you do so, you can create a beautiful high octave note that is in tune and blends with the phrase you are executing.

Always give to the bottom octave notes
Tchaikovsky's "Danse Arabe"

13

LOOKING AHEAD / COMING IN EARLY

Looking ahead and coming in early (when reading music) are essential in flute artistry. Most players hold the note they are playing with their eye which makes forward motion impossible. This type of holding is especially destructive when playing long to short moves. The eye, paralyzed by the long note, holds onto it for too long and then suddenly moves over to the short note at the last second, crashing down upon it. Much like a baseball player who swings late at a pitch, flutists constantly move late to the upcoming short note. The key to overcoming this problem is a simple one: *as soon as you play the long note, immediately move your eye over to the short note, and begin it before its time.* Despite the fact that this process is a simple one, it is exceedingly difficult to do at first, because your eye has been stuck looking at the long note for so long. You must learn to move your eye over to the short note *as soon as you touch the long note you are playing.* Phil used to summarize this idea as "play and get off."

Coming in early eliminates the holding sound in your playing, gives you forward motion, and stops you from "landing" on a note, which destroys its freedom. All of your notes should move in individual lengths, like the waves in the ocean, in constant motion, connected by your flowing airstream. There is a completely different quality of sound created when you move through a note as opposed to holding it. Phil would constantly complain to me, "Why are you staring at a note you've already played while ignoring the next one?"

Looking ahead also helps you identify the next note in terms of whether it is a color note, open or closed, etc., and will make you a much better sight-reader as well. When you walk down the street, you do not stare at the ground; you keep your head up and look forward. As a flutist, you can do the same by letting go of the long note you are playing (with your eye) while moving all of your attention to the upcoming short one.

NOTE: As long as you are looking ahead at the short note, *you are free to play the long note for as long as you want to.*

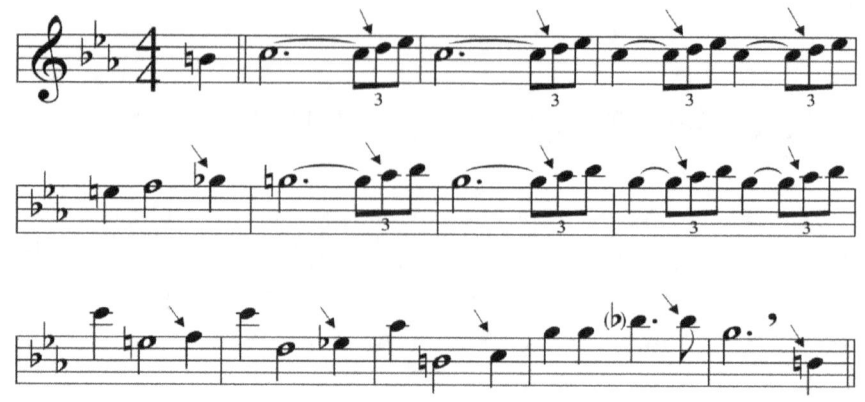

**Ex. of looking ahead / coming in early
on "Moonlight Serenade"**

NOTE: Syncopation is another example where using the "coming in early" idea will be of great benefit. Most players drag when they play a syncopated phrase, because they do not look ahead to the next note. When you play a syncopated phrase, *move to the next note earlier than you think you should.* This will free your sound and create the correct tempo and feel for the syncopation, and will keep your flute bell alive and ringing.

Ex. of syncopation on "Brahms' 3rd"

A final advantage to looking ahead and coming early is when you play a phrase with a series of rests. It is very difficult to once again not drag or "stop and start" in this situation, so the key is to look *past the rest* and to come in early with the next note. Pay no attention to the rest but instead, move your eye to the upcoming note after it. In this way, you will be able to continue to flow through the phrase, without stopping your air. I liken this to a stream that flows downwards, both in and around and over and under the rocks that try to impede it. Your air, fingers and eyes are the stream while the rests are the rocks. Do not let them stop you from flowing through them and you will be successful.

Ex. of playing through rests on "Beethoven's 9th"

14

MAGNETIZING

Magnetizing is a very important part of flute artistry. It occurs whenever you play a note on the downbeat. The idea is *to lean on the downbeat a little bit more than the other notes in the phrase*, so that the ear is drawn towards it, which will give you a better rhythmic shape to your phrasing.

Magnetizing is also extremely effective when you play a series of notes that have the same rhythm. If you magnetize the downbeats, you will make it much easier for people playing beside you to follow you, because they can feel that extra strength in your downbeats. This is a critical part of your playing as without it, you will have no pulse in your phrasing, which will make all of your notes feel and sound the same.

Ex. of magnetizing the first note of each group

NOTE: Sometimes, based on the phrase you are playing, you do not need to magnetize all of the downbeats. You must analyze each and every phrase you play and decide, based on its rhythm, which downbeats to magnetize.

15

BEGINNINGS & ENDINGS

This idea explores the way you begin and end your phrases with your airstream. The idea is to always begin and end *in the bottom of the flute.* No matter what the first or last note of the phrase is, visualize its placement at the end of the flute. That way, if you start on a high D, for example, see the D starting in the deepest part of the flute, which will send your air downwards and stop you from squeezing or forcing the note out. Similarly, when you end a phrase, allow the last note to sink to the bottom of the flute, where true pitch and the bottom vibration of every note comes from. This is a very simple process but one that very few flutists use. Most of the time when a flutist starts on a high note, the flute is raised into the air while the flutist, grimacing with supposed intensity and feeling, blasts the note out of the instrument to the heavens. Because of this, the warmth, depth and pitch of the note is obliterated. However, if you can adjust your way of thinking and deliver your beginning and ending notes "downstairs," you can create the bottom sound in your playing. *Always begin and end your phrases in the bell!*

PART THREE:
THE CEREBRAL & THE HEART

16
INTERPRETATION

Interpretation, or how we tell the story, is an interesting, creative part of flute artistry. Because there are so many creative choices you can make, how you interpret anything you play is an extremely personal matter between *you and the song*. Now that the positioning and technical aspects of your training are in place, you can focus on expressing your feelings and emotions. While there is no one way to interpret a melody, there are some fundamental ideas I have found to be extremely helpful. Ultimately, it is up to you to decide how you will deliver your songs to the audience, but if you are passionate about the material, understand it thoroughly, and follow your heart, you have a great chance for success.

Your first step of interpretation should always consist of *dissecting the song through the four cornerstones*. It is your obligation to *serve your flute first*, before anything else. The four cornerstones approach will enable you to master the sound of the piece, after which you can add your feelings and emotions to complete the process. From an interpretative standpoint, you must decide the length of every entrance note, bottom note, first short note after a long note, closed to open note, and any other notes you deem important to the telling of the story.

The second step is *to use an adjective or simple idea to describe the nature of the song*. This gives you a clear picture of how you want the piece to sound and feel. As an example, when I recorded John Barry's "Body Heat" theme, I used "mysterious" as my description. Once in the studio, it was a fascinating process to try and create that particular sound and feeling. Even a simple love song can be thought of in many different ways: tenderness, longing, painful, etc. Find the best description for the song, create the appropriate quality of sound to match it, and you will be successful.

Another component of interpretation is to decide *what kind of articulation the song requires*. Although this may seem straight forward, many flute players are not creative in this respect, deciding instead to simply follow the instructions on the page. Flutists also suffer from a common woodwind problem that I call "tonguitis," that being, over-tonguing everything they play. My approach is to do the opposite, and to be *as smooth and flowing as possible* with my articulation. The bottom line is that you must decide, *phrase by phrase*, what the best articulation is to serve the story. Every song is unique and should be treated as such. Experiment with different articulations until you find what works best. It goes without saying that if the song is written well, the articulations should be easy for you to interpret. A Sousa march demands a tongued, accented articulation; an Irving Berlin love song, a flowing, sensitive, legato touch.

My training with Phil was predicated on, at first, *removing all the articulations in the piece so that everything I played had a legato style.* The only notes he allowed me to tongue were repeated ones. This was a brilliant idea by Phil because it allowed me to devote all of my attention to creating an in-tune, legato sound *first,* before adding any further articulation with the tongue. I strongly recommend this approach and always introduce it to my students.

Choosing the right tempo is another critical factor in interpretation. Unfortunately, almost all musicians act like sheep in a herd, following the tempo set down on the page or copying someone else's tempo that appeals to them. Both of these choices are a mistake for the flute artist. *You must be an individual and find your own tempo for every song you play.* In fact, I will go so far as to say that you must decide the correct tempo *between every finger move you make.* The difference between the right tempo and the wrong one can be miniscule, but is paramount for your success. The tempo you choose must perfectly support your feelings about the song you are playing. Again, think of the waves coming in from the ocean; they move at different speeds and lengths, exactly as your tempo should in your phrases. Don't be a machine – be flexible, rhythmical, and always serve the story you are telling.

A good example of this is contained in the Hoagy Carmichael song, "Skylark." Playing this beautiful piece in one tempo destroys its inherent qualities. The first phrase starts with two high C's followed by a bottom note Bb, which leads to a high Eb. Your challenge is to find the exact tempo for that Bb or your high Eb will suffer the consequences. As always, start with stretching and illuminating the Bb and then decide how much of it you need to produce a gorgeous high Eb.

Ex. of choosing the right tempo between notes on "Skylark"

When I first started with Phil he asked me, "Do you have a metronome?" When I told him I did, he barked, "Throw it away – *you're the metronome!*" Sound advice indeed.

The dynamic of the song you are playing is also important in your interpretation. Again, do not blindly follow the instructions on the page. In truth, *every note played should have its own dynamic.* This part of interpretation is often overlooked by flute players, who instead, choose to simply blow loudly through everything they play. This kind of approach is colorless and one-dimensional. Dynamics give your song character and change the feeling or mood of the piece, giving it life and a deeper meaning. Dynamic shading is an integral part of storytelling. Never underestimate the value of its importance to your artistry.

A fantastic example of dynamic shading is to listen to George Michael sing his composition "John and Elvis are Dead." Listen to the way George uses dynamics to tell this haunting, mysterious story. He was an absolute master of storytelling and constantly used dynamic shading when he sang. It is no surprise to me that during his career he sold over 60 million albums and was respected by so many.

Learning the words to the song you are playing is also a key part of interpretation. Not only is it important so that you don't take a breath in the wrong spot (i.e., between "sand" and "wich") but also because the words reveal the story of the song you are playing. Songs like "Charmaine" or "The Song Is Ended" have beautiful lyrics that help the flutist reveal the full story of the song to the listener.

When I was 19 years old and studying with jazz alto saxophone legend Sonny Criss, I learned a crucial lesson from him about this very topic. One day when I arrived at the usual time for a lesson, he asked what song I would like to work on. When I replied, "Stella By Starlight," he immediately asked me: "What are the words, boy?" When I hesitated, he repeated, "Well, what are the words?" When I finally admitted I didn't know them, he became enraged and yelled, "Pack up! Your lesson's over!" Embarrassed, I packed up my horn and headed to the door, but as I was on my way out, he suddenly grabbed me by the arm, glared at me and said: "If you don't know the story, you don't know NOTHIN', boy!" Of course, the master was correct, and since then I have made it a point to study the words to every lyrical song I play, to my great benefit.

Another important part of interpretation is *when and where to use your vibrato.* In general, most flutists overuse their vibrato in the extreme. When they play, they add it like running water through all of their phrases, never turning it off. It is so overdone by most that it becomes nauseating and unbearable to listen to. There seems to be a total disregard for using vibrato as a beautiful, shimmering *addition to your sound*, instead of it dominating everything you play. The only logical reason I can come up with as to why so many in the flute community use vibrato in this way is because they have not been properly trained in this most delicate nuance and therefore cannot turn it on or off at their command. This is indeed unfortunate, because I truly believe that the overdoing of vibrato is the *number one reason listeners turn off from listening to the flute.*

Therefore, I reiterate once again my strongest belief that the vibrato should be used only on long notes, and sparingly. When in doubt as to whether or not to use it, *don't*. The constant use of this incredible flute nuance destroys its value to the listener. You will also need to be able to adjust your vibrato speed to the piece at hand you are playing. A powerful song will require a strong vibrato speed; a tender love song, a gentle vibration. Find your own speeds in your vibrato delivery but, above all, use it sparingly.

NOTE: A fantastic way to examine vibrato that I discovered, quite by accident, is to study the violin parts of the great symphonies. When I started playing along with these incredible pieces of music, I was stunned by the use of vibrato the violins delivered. The amount of vibrato the violins used changed constantly, to great effect, always based on the particular emotion and feeling of *each and every phrase*. Again, most flutists overuse and overdo vibrato with no relief, which is a mistake. Study the violins and their expert use of vibrato and you will derive great benefit from doing so.

Nuance and subtlety are also critical components of interpretation. Nuance (the subtle change in feeling or expression) and subtlety (a change so delicate it is almost impossible to describe) are very closely aligned to each other and help bring the song you are playing to life. *Every phrase of every song you play must reflect these two elements.* The nuance of how long you rest on a note, for example, is critical to your success; the subtlety of a particular kind of softness you use to play a love song also helps in revealing the essence of the song to the listener. Do not simply blow at one volume and play at one speed, but instead, follow your heart to discover the nuances and subtleties inherent in the pieces you play.

The final component of interpretation is *phrasing,* defined as "how we tell the story." There are really no fixed laws re phrasing, except that it must be *your personal form of expression.* All correct phrasing targets one goal and one goal only: *providing the listener with your honest, intimate feelings of the song you are playing.* When you go to see a film, you do not see the director, but instead, *see his vision of the story.* The flutist is no different. You must, through your phrasing, present a "sound picture" of the story you are telling that represents your deepest, most personal commitment and understanding of it; the listener is vicariously counting on you to do so. Your expertise at phrasing will be the difference between moving the listener or leaving them cold. *Find songs you are passionate for and phrase them from the heart out* – that is my sincerest recommendation.

As the exceptional violinist and teacher Leopold Auer wrote in his masterful book, Violin Playing As I Teach It, "All really beautiful phrasing depends, of course, on technical perfection. For no matter how fine the student's musical instinct and his sense of proportion may be, faulty bowing – and faulty fingering as well – will inevitably destroy the continuity which is the very essence of smooth and convincing phrasing, and result in misrepresentation of the composer's ideas and intentions. Without technical competence even the most gifted interpretative instinct must fail of practical application."

In other words, play from your heart, but don't forget your air and fingers!

Summarizing our chapter, interpretation is a combined effort of the four cornerstones, understanding the song, articulation, tempo, rhythm, dynamics, lyrics, vibrato, nuance, subtlety, phrasing, and technical perfection. All of these processes are like spokes on a wheel; they must be lined up in conjunction with each other or the piece will not flow. And with regards to interpretation on the flute, I once again offer this suggestion: do not follow the herd and try to fit in by playing the same material other flutists do, but instead, build your repertoire based on the pieces that *move you, capture your heart, and inspire your imagination.*

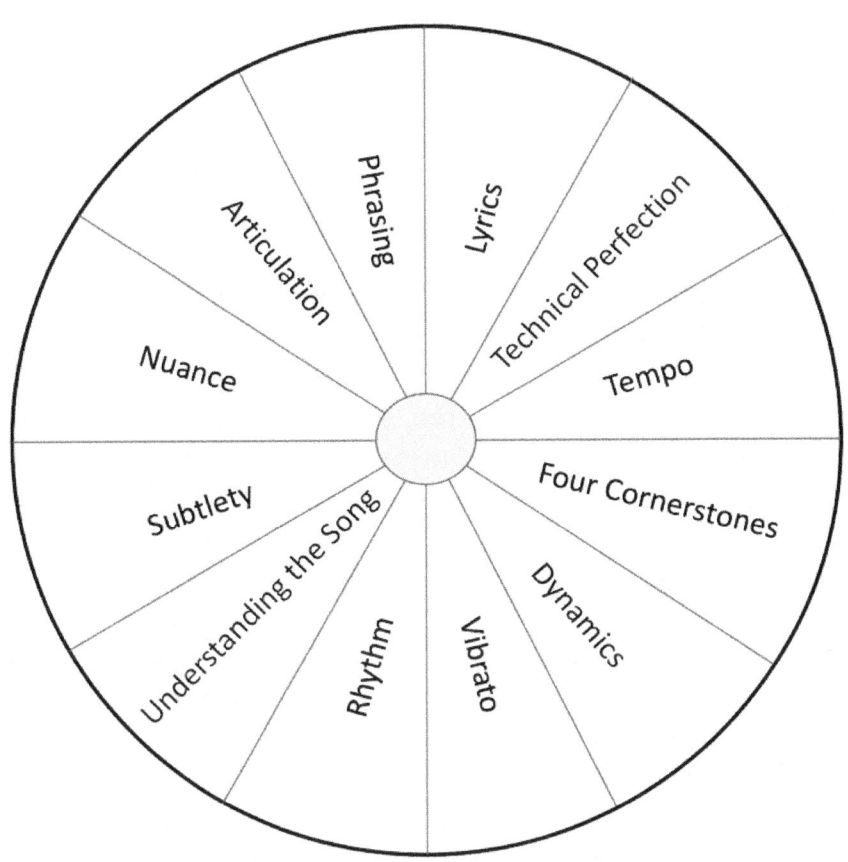

Ex. of interpretation as "spokes on a wheel"

17

IMPROVISATION

Improvisation is the spontaneous art of revealing your innermost, private, passionate feelings about the song you are playing. It is a completely personal experience. Imagine someone puts a piece of paper in front of you with some crayons and asks you to draw whatever you like. *That is improvisation.* No two people will draw exactly the same image with the same color choices. There are also no steadfast rules re improvisation. Some people will play all the right notes in their solo, while others will deliberately play notes that arrest the ear of the listener. As improvisation is a personal choice and therefore subjective, it cannot be judged or graded. Therefore, the number one rule of improvisation is to *find yourself and your feelings when you improvise.*

Choosing songs you are passionate for is critical in improvisation. Find the songs that stir and touch your heart, and you will find it easier to improvise on them. Be an individual and make your own choices; this will distinguish you as an artist. Feel free to explore any and all types of songs to improvise on. Many improvisers pick an idiom such as jazz, pop, or rock, and stick to that one style only, but you have the entire world of music to draw from, with no boundaries.

As an example of this, on one of my jazz albums, I recorded "Caruso," a famous operatic song. It was a fantastic challenge to try and honor the original feeling of the song, while at the same time adding a touch of improvisation to it. Choose any song that speaks to you, and you will have a greater opportunity for success.

Memorizing the melody is also a very helpful tool for improvisation. This allows you to close your eyes and go into yourself, without visual distraction. When the eyes close, the ears open and sensitivity increases, which can only help in the improvisatory process. Another benefit to memorizing the melody is that there are times when we draw a blank during our improvisation, but if you have the melody at your fingertips, you can draw from it until your ideas return.

Studying the scales and chords of the song you are improvising on is a must; scales give you a note by note breakdown of every chord you are improvising on, while the chords give you the specific notes the rhythm section plays. Saturate yourself with both of these as they are the building blocks of your improvisation. That said, it is important to remember scales and chords are not the end-all of your solo; they represent only a part of the improvisatory process.

Play-along recordings are a great tool for improvisation. Playing along with a rhythm section enables you to thoroughly immerse yourself in both the song and the harmony it presents. Even if you cannot read music or do not know chords or scales, if you can find something to play that matches what the rhythm section is playing, you have a solo. Another advantage play-along recordings present is the chance for you to sing a solo along with the rhythm section. Whatever you sing is what you should play, as it comes from within you and is the most natural form of improvising. As Jamey Aebersold (the pioneer of play-along recordings) once said at a clinic of his I attended, "The best solo you play is the one you sing in the shower!"

Interpreting the style of the song is also important in improvising. Playing on "Ornithology" requires using the bebop language when you improvise, while the ballad "Moonlight In Vermont" requires a completely different approach. Avoid playing every solo the same way as this will bore the listener. The only reason I mention this is because so many players disregard this idea, which puzzles me to no end. As the old saying goes, "Variety is the spice of life." Every song and solo you play should have a different feeling, and if the song is well written, it should be easy to interpret what kind of feeling you want your solo to reflect.

Use space when you solo. The universe is made up of mostly space; consider this idea when you improvise. Miles Davis said, "It's not the notes you play – it's the notes you leave out." Improvisers who jam up every single bit of space with endless notes and licks can make it difficult for the listener to absorb and keep up with their solo. Of course, there are some notable exceptions; John Coltrane instantly comes to mind. However, if you can add rhythmic diversity to your soloing, you can offer beginnings and endings to your ideas, which should make it easier for the listener to relate to.

Try to hear something before you start improvising. So many players immediately start soloing, without first allowing the listening process inside of them to take effect. True improvisation occurs at the moment, even if you have a general idea of what you are going to play. Listening before you start also allows you to feed off what the rhythm section is doing. An improvised solo is a team concept, not an individual one. If you think that way, you will be surprised how much the accompanying musicians can help you to create moments of beauty and meaning when you improvise.

I was fortunate to work beside a great drummer for over 20 years. When we would play live, we would oftentimes trade solos on tunes. I was always amazed and inspired by his rhythmic ideas and would try to answer them, which was not only great fun but true, spontaneous improvisation.

If you play something you like, repeat it. You do not have to come up with something new on every phrase you improvise! *Repetition is exceedingly attractive to the listener.* If you play something that interests you, explore it as thoroughly as you can. I always think of the first movement of Beethoven's 5th Symphony, where the great master took two four-note phrases and worked them over and over, through repetition, to great effect. Follow Beethoven's example and use repetiton in your improvising.

Try the inside- outside technique of improvising. The idea behind this is to go outside the chord by a half-step and then resolve back to the original chord. This creates an interesting inside-outside sound that appeals to the ear because of the tension it momentarily creates.

Ex. of "inside / outside" technique

Explore the entire range of the flute when improvising. Most flutists stay in the top register of the flute when soloing. Try using the middle and bottom registers as well, as this will present a varied approach to the sound of your solos, and make you more interesting to the listener.

NOTE: The flute is not a strong instrument in its lower register. Middle C, for example, has less than half the sonority of a violin. However, that should not discourage you from using it (or any other low notes) in your improvisation because they have a special sound quality that is both haunting and captivating.

Find your own way of improvising. Yes, we should study and learn from the master improvisers and incorporate some of their ideas into our solos, but simply copying them is not artistic or genuine. Emulate but don't copy – *find yourself when you improvise.*

Changing the melody is also an important part of improvising. The standard approach is to play the melody of a song, take a solo, and then return to the melody. The first time you present the melody, honor the composer by playing it *exactly as written.* After your solo is complete, return to the melody but *change it ever so slightly.* This will make the melody sound fresh and new for the listener.

The master of this approach was Frank Sinatra. Whenever he sang the melody for the second time, he would always change it. He had perfect taste in this regard and brought new life and interest to the song he was singing through the small changes he would implement. Study the many recordings Sinatra left behind and learn the value of this simple yet brilliant process.

Theme and variation is a very helpful tool for improvisation. We are sometimes put in a position where we are asked to improvise on a song we are not familiar with. One way to surmount this problem is to "hug the melody." As soon as you change *one note or rhythm of a song,* you have an improvisation. Adding a few rhythmic ideas or variations to the melody creates interest for the listener. In classical music, Mozart, Beethoven and Brahms were experts at this, doing it repeatedly in their compositions. Study

71

these gifted artists and consider adding theme and variation to your improvisations.

Draw from your life experiences when improvising. When playing a painful love song, for example, your improvisation will be more personal and honest if you reveal to the listener the particular memories, feelings and experiences you felt when you went through a loss of this nature. Many actors use this technique as well. Oftentimes, they arrive on the set in a jubilant state of mind, yet their first scene requires them to break down and cry. In order to conquer this, they use memories of something painful from their past to "bring up the tears" from within. The flutist can do the same with great effect. Of course, this implies that you have experienced these kinds of emotions; many young players have not yet suffered lost love or pain, so they have no way of accessing these kinds of feelings for their solo. This is why most improvisers improve with age; the more excruciating losses you have weathered, the more you have to draw from. The great arranger Nelson Riddle revealed that Sinatra did truly not learn to sing ballads until his tumultuous marriage to Ava Gardner had fallen apart; one of my own extremely gifted students who completed his training with me said, "Now all I have to do is fall in love and get crushed." Draw from your life experiences in your improvisation and you will connect to the song and the listener in the deepest way possible.

In conclusion, improvisation is much more than being a technician and playing the correct chord notes and scales. It is revealing to the listener *your personal feelings* about the song you are playing. It is an in-depth, honest account of the relationship between you and the song. When improvising on "Charmaine," for example, thinking about what chords and scales to use is important, but far more important is the vision you have of Charmaine: her eyes, her smile, the pain of losing her, of wondering if she will come back to you (as the story of the song reveals). Improvising is storytelling in its most intimate form because it comes *directly from your heart.*

The listener is expecting this from you, to vicariously feed off of the emotions you provide. Without your emotions providing the essence of your solos, you will at best move a few people, but not many. And with regard to this, I offer a simple idea: *only select songs to improvise on that captivate you and fill you with deep feeling and emotion.*

CODA

Phil used to always tell me, "The first lesson is the same as the last lesson." This is a brilliant concept because it reveals that the process of playing the flute *remains the same every time we pick up the instrument.* Our position is forward and balanced, our air flows through the flute to the bell, and our fingers are timed through expert open and closed execution. These three elements are the foundation of our playing and never change. It is only our *mastery of them* that is left for us to pursue. Since first meeting Phil some 47 years ago, I find myself still working on perfecting these elements, both as a performer and a teacher, with tremendous passion, interest, and curiosity.

In general, the flutists of today disregard these fundamental building blocks and instead, replace them with the overuse of emotion. They dance around like the Pied Piper, making the music they are playing a visual performance instead of an audio one. Yes, it goes without saying that the visual world of music is now more prevalent than ever, but we should be careful not to let it destroy our quality of sound. I find it hard to imagine Rampal or Heifetz dancing around while playing their instruments. As Heifetz said after being criticized for never showing any emotion during his performances, "Why should I smile when no-one past the first few rows in the audience will even be able to see me?"

And so I would like to offer this advice as a mediation between these two completely opposite components of flute artistry: learn to play the flute from the inside out with the four cornerstones, develop the exact kind of quality of sound you want in your playing, and then and only then introduce whatever visual stimulus you feel you need to enhance your performance. When you are in the studio, you only have your sound to concentrate on; live performances have a different dynamic and feel to them. Find what works for you but *never betray your sound;* that is my advice.

I remember watching the incredible alto saxophonist Sonny Criss play at a live concert shortly before his death. Sonny stood in a forward, relaxed position and never moved his body *one inch* while playing, as the most angelic, heartfelt sound imaginable poured out of him through his instrument. At another concert, I heard another fantastic saxophonist perform, and despite the fact that he rocked back and forth while playing, his artistry was so disciplined that his body movement did not interfere in the least with his stunning technique and quality of sound.

Shortly before Phil passed, I called him and asked, "What are you working on these days?" to which he replied, "A to B, pal – A to B." The first lesson is the same as the last lesson. In honor of that, I enclose the notes from my first lesson with Phil for your perusal and education.

NOVEMBER 16, 1978

Position – forward and balanced

Foot, finger and teeth up in preparation for entrance note

Air to bell – steady and uninterrupted through top teeth

Fingers timed through open and closed

Air meets fingers

Fingers in tune with the pearls

Leave throat open – face alone – just the air circulating properly

Don't help the horn play – stay out of the way with your body

The louder you play, the less the ear will hear

Rest an instant longer on all the keys to recognize the pearl and the key

No note should be a surprise

When the air meets the finger at the key, nothing can happen to interrupt the sound

THE PHIL ANGEL

Several years ago, a very young student came to me for a lesson. She had traveled from China to Vancouver for the summer and somehow found her way to me. A time was arranged and she arrived in my studio. As usual, I gave her the same piece of music I give all my first-time students and prepared to introduce her my ideas and methods. As she was only eight or nine years old, I assumed I would have a lot of teaching to do in the lesson.

However, as soon as she started playing, I was transfixed. Her quality of sound was angelic; her fingers were glued to the keys with flawless open and closed technique, and her interpretation was both inspiring and uniquely her own. Moreover, she luxuriated the bottom notes, took relaxed, full breaths, and her positioning was forward and still.

After she finished playing the piece to perfection, I was in shock. I asked her, "How did you do that?" to which she replied, "I don't know." I suddenly realized that there was nothing I could teach her, that this young child could already do what had taken me decades to try to absorb and perfect in my own playing.

As I sat there stunned, she played for a little while longer and then she said, "I want to come back and study with you all summer," which of course, delighted me.

Strangely, I never saw her again. She disappeared as quickly as she had come, in a flash. I found myself wondering, was she even real, or had I just imagined her?

Many years and many students have come my way since that mysterious little girl appeared in my studio and played the method perfectly, before I could even teach it to her. She will never be forgotten.

BACK PAGE
FLUTISTS AROUND THE GLOBE:
PREPARE TO BE REVOLUTIONIZED!

This book will reveal the processes of flute artistry as seen through the eyes of three men: Henry Lindeman, Phil Sobel, and Dylan Cramer. Their combined effort spans over 100 years, dating back to the 1920s and continuing to the present day.

Topics in this book will include vibrato, sound production, phrasing, articulation, interpretation, improvisation, nuance, and dynamics, along with the study of the four cornerstones, offered here for the first time to the flute community.

Dylan Cramer has been playing and teaching the flute for five decades. He has recorded six albums and is currently working on his seventh. Along with his playing career he teaches flute, saxophone, clarinet, violin, and piano. This is his third book.

www.dylancramer.com